SCHOLASTIC

Writing Lessons to Meet the Common Core

Grade 4

Linda Ward Beech

NEW YORK ● TORONTO ● LONDON ● AUCKLAND ● SYDNEY
MEXICO CITY ● NEW DELHI ● HONG KONG ● BUENOS AIRES

Teaching
Resources

Cover design by Scott Davis
Interior design by Kathy Massaro
Image credits: page 9 (left) © iStockphoto.com/Martin_Adams2000, (right) © iStockphoto.com/parameter;
page 30 (left) © Jakub Krechowicz/Big Stock Photo. All images © 2013.
Illustrations by Teresa Anderko, Constanza Basaluzzo, Hector Borlasca, Maxie Chambliss, Rusty Fletcher,
Aleksey and Olga Ivanov, Anthony Lewis

ISBN: 978-0-545-49599-8

1 2 3 4 5 6 7 8 9 10   40   20 19 18 17 16 15 14 13

Contents

About This Book

. . . .

To build a foundation for college and career readiness, students need to learn to use writing as a way of offering and supporting opinions, demonstrating understanding of the subjects they are studying, and conveying real and imagined experiences and events. They learn to appreciate that a key purpose of writing is to communicate clearly to an external, sometimes unfamiliar audience, and they begin to adapt the form and content of their writing to accomplish a particular task and purpose.

—COMMON CORE STATE STANDARDS FOR ENGLISH LANGUAGE ARTS, JUNE 2010

This book includes step-by-step instructions for teaching the three forms of writing—Opinion, Informative/Explanatory, and Narrative—covered in the Common Core State Standards (CCSS). The CCSS are a result of a state-led effort to establish a single set of clear educational standards aimed at providing students nationwide with a high-quality education. The standards outline the knowledge and skills that students should achieve during their years in school.

The writing standards are a subset of the Common Core English Language Arts Standards. They provide "a focus for instruction" to help students gain a mastery of a range of skills and applications necessary for writing clear prose. This book is divided into three main sections; each section includes six lessons devoted to one of the writing forms covered in the CCSS for grade 4. You'll find more about each of these types of writing on pages 6–7.

- **Lessons 1–6** (pages 8–25) focus on the standards for writing opinion pieces.
- **Lessons 7–12** (pages 26–43) emphasize standards particular to informative/explanatory writing. (Lesson 7 focuses on the important skill of summarizing and paraphrasing information in research notes.)
- **Lessons 13–18** (pages 44–61) address the standards for narrative writing.

Although the CCSS do not specify how to teach any form of writing, the lessons in this book follow the gradual release of responsibility model of instruction: I Do It, We Do It, You Do It (Pearson & Gallagher, 1983). This model provides educators with a framework for releasing responsibility to students in a gradual manner. It recognizes that we learn best when a concept is demonstrated to us; when we have sufficient time to practice it with support; and when we are then given the opportunity to try it on our own. Each phase is equally important, but the chief goal is to teach for independence—the You Do It phase—so that students really learn to take over the skill and apply it in new situations.

Pearson, P. D., & Gallagher, M. C. (1983). "The Instruction of Reading Comprehension." *Contemporary Educational Psychology*, 8 (3).

A Look at the Lessons

The lessons in each section progress in difficulty and increase in the number of objectives and standards covered. This format enables you to use beginning or later lessons in a section depending on your students' abilities. Each lesson begins with a list of the objectives and standards. A general reproducible assessment checklist of standards for each writing form appears at the end of the book. (See pages 62–64.)

Here's a look at the features in each lesson.

Lesson Page 1

The first page is the teaching page of each lesson. It provides a step-by-step plan for using the student reproducible on the second lesson page and the On Your Own activity on the third lesson page. The teaching page closely follows the organization of the student reproducibles. This page also models sample text that students might generate when completing page 2 of the lesson. Finally, the teaching page includes an opportunity for students to review their classmates' work using the reproducible assessment checklist customized to the lesson's writing form. Each checklist also reminds students to check for correct punctuation, spelling, and paragraph form.

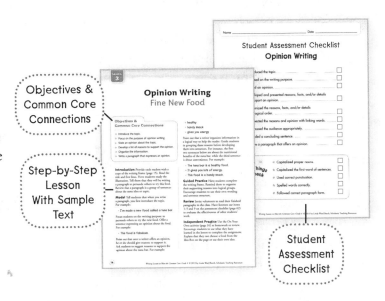

Objectives & Common Core Connections

Step-by-Step Lesson With Sample Text

Student Assessment Checklist

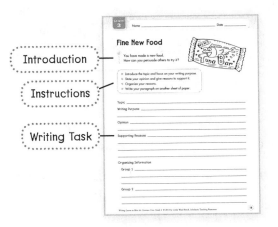

Introduction

Instructions

Writing Task

Lesson Page 2

The second page is a student reproducible, which is the core of the lesson. Students complete this writing frame as you guide them. In most lessons, students use the completed page as the basis for a paragraph they write on a separate sheet of paper.

Although you provide a model for completing this reproducible, you'll want to encourage students to use their own ideas, words, and sentences as much as possible.

Lesson Page 3

The third page is a writing frame for independent work. It follows a format similar to the one students used for the first reproducible. Students choose their topic from the suggested list or use their own idea. In most lessons, students use the completed page as the basis for a paragraph they write on a separate sheet of paper.

Introduction

Topic Suggestions

Writing Task

Three Forms of Writing

The CCSS focus on three forms of writing—opinion, informative/explanatory, and narrative.

Opinion Pieces (Standards W.4.1, W.4.1a, W.4.1b, W.4.1c, W.4.1d)

The purpose of writing opinion pieces is to convince others to think or act in a certain way, to encourage readers or listeners to share the writer's point of view, beliefs, or position. Opinion pieces are also known as persuasive writing.

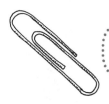

I think a paper clip is a clever invention.

In developing an opinion piece, students must learn to introduce the topic, present a point of view, and supply valid reasons, facts, and expert opinions to support it. Phrases such as *I think, I believe, you should/should not* all signal persuasive writing.

This food is fabulous.

When teaching these lessons, display different examples of opinion pieces. You might include:

- editorials
- book, movie, TV, and theater reviews
- print advertisements
- letters to the editor
- letters of appeal
- feature columns

As students learn to produce different forms of writing, they are also enhancing their ability to recognize these forms in their reading.

Informative/Explanatory Writing (Standards W.4.2, W.4.2a, W.4.2b, W.4.2c, W.4.2d, W.4.2e)

The purpose of informative/explanatory writing is to inform the reader by giving facts, explanations, and other information. Informative/explanatory writing is also called expository writing.

When writing an informative/explanatory piece, students must introduce the topic and give facts, details, descriptions, and other information about the topic. The information should also be organized in a logical way. Many kinds of informative/explanatory writing require research. Sometimes illustrations are included with informative/explanatory pieces.

The bald eagle is a symbol of the United States.

Display different examples of informative/explanatory writing. You might include:

- reports
- news articles
- how-to articles
- biographies
- directions
- textbooks
- magazines
- recipes

The outside of a teepee is made from a buffalo hide.

Writing Lessons to Meet the Common Core: Grade 4 © 2013 by Linda Ward Beech, Scholastic Teaching Resources

Narrative Writing (Standards W.4.3, W.4.3a, W.4.3b, W.4.3c, W.4.3d, W.4.3e)

The purpose of narrative writing is to entertain. A narrative gives an account or a story. Usually, a narrative tells about something that happens over a period of time. Narratives can be true or imaginary.

He dreamed he was riding on a whale.

When working on a narrative, students must develop a real or imagined experience or event. They must also establish a situation, or plot and setting, create characters, and recount events in a chronological sequence. Narratives usually include descriptive details. Many include dialogue.

Mrs. Bean's shoes decided to go for a walk without her.

"It was here all along. Phew!"

When introducing narrative writing, display different examples. You might include:

- stories
- mysteries
- fables
- folktales
- myths
- science fiction
- friendly letters

Additional Writing Standards

Although this book focuses on the forms of writing called for in the CCSS, you can also incorporate the standards that relate to the production and distribution of writing and research to build and present knowledge. These standards include:

- W.4.4 Produce writing in which the development and organization are appropriate to task and purpose.

- W.4.5 Develop and strengthen writing as needed by planning, revising, and editing.

- W.4.6 Use technology to produce and publish writing and to interact with others; use keyboarding skills.

- W.4.7 Conduct short research projects that build knowledge about a topic.

- W.4.8 Recall relevant information from experiences or gather information from print and digital sources. Take notes and categorize information and provide sources.

- W.4.9 Draw evidence from informational texts to support analysis, reflection, and research.

- W.4.10 Write routinely over extended time frames allowing for research, reflection, and revision.

Language Standards

You can also incorporate the CCSS Language Standards that focus on the conventions of standard English grammar and usage when writing or speaking (L.4.1); the conventions of standard English capitalization, punctuation, and spelling (L.4.2); and the knowledge of language conventions when writing, speaking, reading, or listening (L.4.3).

Writing Lessons to Meet the Common Core: Grade 4 © 2013 by Linda Ward Beech, Scholastic Teaching Resources

Opinion Writing
Pick a Planet

Objectives & Common Core Connections

* Introduce the topic.
* Focus on the purpose of opinion writing.
* State an opinion about the topic.
* Develop a list of facts to support the opinion.

Introduction Provide each student with a copy of the writing frame (page 9). Read the title and first lines. Draw attention to the images. Ask students to form an opinion about which planet they would prefer to visit. Tell them that they will be writing to persuade others to agree with their opinion. Remind students that an opinion is a point of view or what someone thinks or believes about something.

Model Tell students that in an opinion piece, writers should introduce the topic. Write the topic in sentence form on the board. For example:

* It would be fun to visit another planet.

Call on a volunteer to tell what planet he or she would choose. For example:

* I think we should visit Mars.

Remind students that they are writing to persuade their readers to agree with them. Ask: *How do you persuade someone to agree with you?* Help students understand that a writer might give facts to support an opinion. Brainstorm some facts or have some relevant research materials available and invite students to research facts that support the opinion. For example:

* closer to Earth
* spacecraft landed there
* has interesting canyons

Coach students in developing complete sentences based on the reasons. For example:

* Earth is closer to Mars than to Jupiter.
* Spacecraft have already landed there.
* The planet has interesting canyons.

Guided Practice Have students complete the writing frame. Remind them to introduce the topic, focus on the purpose of writing about the topic, state an opinion, list facts to support their opinion, and write some practice sentences. Encourage students to use their own wording and sentence structure. If students choose to visit Jupiter, guide them in developing facts to support their opinion.

Review Invite volunteers to read their finished pages to the class. Have listeners use items 1–4 on the assessment checklist (page 62) to evaluate the effectiveness of other students' work.

Independent Practice Use the On Your Own activity (page 10) as homework or review. Encourage students to use what they have learned in the lesson to complete the assignment. Explain that they can choose a place in the solar system from the Idea Box or use their own idea. Have appropriate reference materials and a computer with Internet access available for student research.

Name _____ Date _____

Pick a Planet

Mars

Jupiter

⭐ Which planet would you like to visit?
How can you get others to agree with you?

- Introduce the topic.
- Focus on your writing purpose.
- State your opinion.
- List facts to support your opinion.
- Write some practice sentences.

Topic _____

_____

Writing Purpose _____

_____

Opinion _____

_____

Supporting Facts _____

_____

_____

_____

Practice Sentences _____

_____

_____

_____

_____

_____

_____

_____

Name _____ Date _____

On Your Own

Which place in the solar system would you like to visit? Choose one from the Idea Box or think of your own idea. Then, complete this page to get others to agree with you.

Idea Box

○ Mercury   ○ Venus   ○ Neptune

○ My Idea: _____

Topic _____

_____

Writing Purpose _____

_____

Opinion _____

_____

Supporting Facts _____

_____

_____

Practice Sentences _____

_____

_____

_____

_____

_____

Opinion Writing
Design Project

Objectives & Common Core Connections

* Introduce the topic.
* Focus on the purpose of opinion writing.
* State an opinion about the topic.
* Develop a list of reasons with details to support the opinion.

Introduction Provide each student with a copy of the writing frame (page 12). Read the title and first lines. Have students read the captions and study the picture. Ask students to think of other things they might say about the bandana. Tell them that they will be writing to persuade others to agree with their opinion. Remind students that an opinion is a point of view or what someone thinks or believes about something.

Model Tell students that in an opinion piece, writers should introduce the topic. Write the topic in sentence form on the board. For example:

* I designed this bandana.

Call on a volunteer to suggest what the designer's opinion about the bandana might be. For example:

* I think it is very original.

Remind students that they are writing to persuade their readers to agree with them. Ask: *How do you persuade someone to agree with you?* Help students recall that they should offer reasons. Point out that a writer can make reasons stronger and more persuasive by including details. For example:

* fun to wear
* good looking
* colorful polka dots draw attention

Encourage students to come up with other reasons, then talk about the different reasons and how they might be useful in persuading someone to think the bandana is great. Coach students in developing complete sentences from the reasons. For example:

* This bandana will be fun to wear.
* It's very good looking.
* The colorful polka dots will draw attention.

Guided Practice Have students complete the writing frame. Remind them to introduce the topic, focus on the purpose of writing, state an opinion, list reasons with details to support their opinion, and write some practice sentences. Encourage students to use their own wording and sentence structure.

Review Invite volunteers to read their finished pages to the class. Have listeners use items 1–4 on the assessment checklist (page 62) to evaluate the effectiveness of other students' work.

Independent Practice Use the On Your Own activity (page 13) as homework or review. Encourage students to use what they have learned in the lesson to complete the assignment. Explain that they can choose a design project from the Idea Box or use their own idea. Provide paper so students can draw a picture of their design before they begin writing about it.

Writing Lessons to Meet the Common Core: Grade 4 © 2013 by Linda Ward Beech, Scholastic Teaching Resources

Name _____ Date _____

Design Project

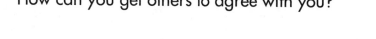

It's wild!

It's perfect!

You designed a new bandana and think it's great.
How can you get others to agree with you?

- Introduce the topic.
- Focus on your writing purpose.
- State your opinion.
- List reasons with details to support your opinion.
- Write some practice sentences.

Topic _____

_____

Writing Purpose _____

_____

Opinion _____

_____

Supporting Reasons/Details _____

_____

_____

Practice Sentences _____

_____

_____

_____

_____

_____

Writing Lessons to Meet the Common Core: Grade 4 © 2013 by Linda Ward Beech, Scholastic Teaching Resources

On Your Own

What would you like to design? Choose something from the Idea Box or think of your own idea. Draw a picture of your design. Then, complete this page to persuade others to agree that your design is great.

Idea Box

○ Sweatshirt   ○ Cap   ○ Book Cover   ○ My Idea:

_____

_____

Topic _____

_____

Writing Purpose _____

_____

Opinion _____

_____

Supporting Reasons/Details _____

_____

_____

Practice Sentences _____

_____

_____

_____

_____

Opinion Writing
Fine New Food

Objectives & Common Core Connections

* Introduce the topic.
* Focus on the purpose of opinion writing.
* State an opinion about the topic.
* Develop a list of reasons to support the opinion.
* Organize the information.
* Write a paragraph that expresses an opinion.

Introduction Provide each student with a copy of the writing frame (page 15). Read the title and first lines. Have students study the illustration. Tell them that they will be writing a paragraph to persuade others to try this food. Review that a paragraph is a group of sentences about the same idea or topic.

Model Tell students that when you write a paragraph, you first introduce the topic. For example:

* I've made a new food called a tuna bar.

Focus students on the writing purpose: to persuade others to try the new food. Offer a sentence expressing an opinion about the food. For example:

* This food is fabulous.

Point out that once a writer offers an opinion, he or she should give reasons to support it. Ask students to suggest reasons to support the opinion about the tuna bar. For example:

* healthy
* handy snack
* gives you energy

Point out that a writer organizes information in a logical way to help the reader. Guide students in grouping these reasons before developing them into sentences. For instance, the first two sentences below are about the nutritional benefits of the tuna bar, while the third sentence is about convenience. For example:

* The tuna bar is a healthy food.
* It gives you lots of energy.
* This food is a handy snack.

Guided Practice Have students complete the writing frame. Remind them to organize their supporting reasons into logical groups. Encourage students to use their own wording and sentence structure.

Review Invite volunteers to read their finished paragraphs to the class. Have listeners use items 1–5 and 9 on the assessment checklist (page 62) to evaluate the effectiveness of other students' work.

Independent Practice Use the On Your Own activity (page 16) as homework or review. Encourage students to use what they have learned in the lesson to complete the assignment. Explain that they can choose a food from the Idea Box on the page or use their own idea.

Name _____   Date _____

Fine New Food

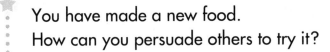

You have made a new food.
How can you persuade others to try it?

- Introduce the topic and focus on your writing purpose.
- State your opinion and give reasons to support it.
- Organize your reasons.
- Write your paragraph on another sheet of paper.

Topic _____

Writing Purpose _____

_____

Opinion _____

_____

Supporting Reasons _____

_____

_____

_____

Organizing Information

Group 1 _____

_____

_____

Group 2 _____

_____

_____

Name _____ Date _____

On Your Own

What new food would you like to make? Choose a food from the Idea Box or think of one of your own. Complete this page. Then, write a paragraph on another sheet of paper to persuade others to agree that your food is great.

Idea Box

○ Eggplant Ice Cream   ○ My Idea: _____

○ Sweet Potato Yogurt   _____

○ Chocolate Lettuce   _____

Topic _____

Writing Purpose _____

_____

Opinion _____

_____

Supporting Reasons _____

_____

_____

_____

Organizing Information

Group 1 _____

_____

_____

Group 2 _____

_____

Opinion Writing
Favorite Author

Objectives & Common Core Connections

* Introduce the topic for a selected audience.
* Focus on the purpose of opinion writing.
* State an opinion about the topic.
* Develop a list of reasons to support the opinion.
* Organize the information.
* Write a paragraph that expresses an opinion.

Introduction Provide each student with a copy of the writing frame (page 18). Read the title and first lines. Have students study the picture. Focus students on the writing purpose: to write a paragraph in which they express an opinion about the author Donald J. Sobol. Explain that students' audience or readers will be other members of the class.

Model Talk about how a writer might engage the class audience by using a friendly, conversational approach in introducing the topic. For example:

* If you like good detective stories, you'll like books by Donald J. Sobol.

Remind students that once a writer offers an opinion, he or she should give reasons to support it. Invite students to suggest possible reasons to support the opinion about Sobol. For example:

* clever plots
* books make me laugh
* good solutions
* learned interesting things

Point out that a writer organizes information in a logical way to help the reader. Guide students in grouping these reasons together and then developing them into sentences. For instance, the first two sentences below are about the writer's reactions to the books, while the third and fourth sentences are about the structure of the books.

* Donald J. Sobol's Encyclopedia Brown books make me laugh.
* I have learned some interesting things from them.

* These books have very clever plots.
* They also have good solutions.

Guided Practice Have students complete the writing frame. Remind them to organize their supporting reasons into logical groups. Encourage students to use their own wording and sentence structure. If students wish to write a different opinion about the author, guide them to develop reasons to support it.

Review Invite volunteers to read their finished paragraphs to the class. Have listeners use items 1–5, 7, and 9 on the assessment checklist (page 62) to evaluate the effectiveness of other students' work.

Independent Practice Use the On Your Own activity (page 19) as homework or review. Encourage students to use what they have learned in the lesson to complete the assignment. Explain that they can choose an author from the Idea Box or write about their own favorite author.

Name _____ Date _____

Favorite Author

Have you ever read the Encyclopedia Brown books?
They are by Donald J. Sobol.

- Introduce the topic with your audience in mind.
- Focus on your writing purpose.
- State your opinion and give reasons to support it.
- Organize your reasons.
- Write your paragraph on another sheet of paper.

Topic _____

Audience _____

Writing Purpose _____

_____

Opinion _____

_____

Supporting Reasons _____

_____

_____

_____

Organizing Information

  Group 1 _____

  _____

  _____

  Group 2 _____

  _____

  _____

Name _____ Date _____

On Your Own

Choose an author from the Idea Box or think of one you really like. Complete this page. Then, write a paragraph on another sheet of paper to persuade your classmates to agree with you.

Idea Box

○ Beverly Cleary   ○ My Idea: _____

○ Jerry Spinelli   _____

○ R.L. Stine   _____

Topic _____

Audience _____

Writing Purpose _____

_____

Opinion _____

_____

Supporting Reasons _____

_____

_____

_____

Organizing Information

Group 1 _____

_____

_____

Group 2 _____

_____

Writing Lessons to Meet the Common Core: Grade 4 © 2013 by Linda Ward Beech, Scholastic Teaching Resources

Opinion Writing
Happy Something Day

Objectives & Common Core Connections

* Introduce the topic for a selected audience.
* Focus on the purpose of opinion writing.
* State an opinion about the topic.
* Develop a list of reasons to support the opinion.
* Organize the information.
* Use linking words to connect the reasons and opinion.
* Write a paragraph that expresses an opinion.

Introduction Provide each student with a copy of the writing frame (page 21). Read the title and first lines. Have students study the illustrations and captions. Explain that they will be writing a paragraph in which they express an opinion about a holiday they make up. Tell students that their audience or readers will be other members of the class.

Model Talk about how a writer might engage the class audience by using a friendly, conversational approach in introducing the topic with an opinion. For example:

* You'll want to celebrate Smile Day every day.

Remind students that once a writer offers an opinion, he or she should give reasons to support it. Invite students to suggest possible reasons to support the opinion about Smile Day. For example:

* you feel good
* make more friends
* easier to get things done
* others feel cheerful

Point out that a writer organizes information in a logical way to help the reader. Guide students in grouping these reasons together and then developing them into sentences. For instance, the first two sentences below are about feelings that smiles produce, while the third and fourth sentences are about outcomes of smiling. Model how ideas can be connected with linking words, such as *in addition* or *for instance*. For example:

* Smiling makes you feel good.
* It makes others feel cheerful, too.
* Smiles make it easier to get things done.
* For instance, it's easier to make friends if you smile at people.

Guided Practice Have students complete the writing frame. Encourage them to use their own wording and sentence structure. If students wish to support the Learn Something New Day instead, help them develop reasons to back their opinion.

Review Invite volunteers to read their finished paragraphs to the class. Have listeners use items 1–7 and 9 on the assessment checklist (page 62) to evaluate the effectiveness of other students' work.

Independent Practice Use the On Your Own activity (page 22) as homework or review. Encourage students to use what they have learned in the lesson to complete the assignment. Explain that they can choose a holiday from the Idea Box or make up one of their own.

Name _____ Date _____

Happy Something Day

You are going to make up a holiday.
What day would you like to celebrate?

Smile Day

- Introduce the topic with your audience in mind. Remember to focus on your writing purpose.
- State your opinion and give reasons to support it.
- Organize your reasons.
- List linking words you might use.
- Write your paragraph on another sheet of paper.

Learn Something New Day

Topic _____

Audience _____

Opinion _____

_____

Supporting Reasons _____

_____

_____

_____

Organizing Information

Group 1 _____

_____

_____

Group 2 _____

_____

_____

Possible Linking Words _____

Name _____ Date _____

On Your Own

What holiday would you like to celebrate? Choose a holiday from the Idea Box or think of one of your own. Complete this page. Then, write a paragraph on another sheet of paper to persuade your classmates to agree with you.

Idea Box

○ Help Others Day   ○ My Idea: _____

○ Read a Book Day   _____

○ Play a Sport Day   _____

Topic _____

Audience _____

Opinion _____

_____

Supporting Reasons _____

_____

_____

_____

Organizing Information

Group 1 _____

_____

_____

Group 2 _____

_____

_____

Possible Linking Words _____

Writing Lessons to Meet the Common Core: Grade 4 © 2013 by Linda Ward Beech, Scholastic Teaching Resources

Opinion Writing
A Great Invention

Objectives & Common Core Connections

* Introduce the topic for a selected audience.
* Focus on the purpose of opinion writing.
* State an opinion about the topic.
* Develop a list of reasons to support the opinion.
* Organize the information.
* Use linking words to connect the reasons and opinion.
* Write a concluding sentence.
* Write a paragraph that expresses an opinion.

Introduction Provide each student with a copy of the writing frame (page 24). Read the title and first line. Have students study the pictures. Explain that students will be writing a paragraph in which they express an opinion about why the safety pin or the paper clip is a great invention. Tell students that their audience or readers will be other members of the class.

Model Talk about how a writer might engage the class audience by using a friendly, conversational approach in introducing the topic with an opinion. For example:

* I think a paper clip is a clever invention with many uses.

Remind students that a writer must give reasons to support an opinion. For example:

* keeps pages together
* bookmark
* money clip
* key ring

Point out that a writer organizes information in a logical way to help the reader. Guide students in grouping these reasons together and then developing them into sentences. For instance, the first two sentences below are about using a paper clip at a desk, while the third and fourth sentences are about more personal uses. Model how ideas can be connected with linking words, such as *in addition* or *for instance*. For example:

* A paper clip holds pieces of paper together.
* You can use it as a bookmark.

* A paper clip makes a good money clip.
* In addition, you can use a paper clip as a key ring.

Explain that a good persuasive paragraph often has a concluding sentence that restates the writer's opinion. For example:

* A paper clip is a very handy item.

Guided Practice Have students complete the writing frame. Encourage them to use their own wording and sentence structure. If students wish to support the safety pin instead, help them develop reasons to back their opinion.

Review Invite volunteers to read their finished paragraphs to the class. Have listeners use items 1–9 on the assessment checklist (page 62) to evaluate the effectiveness of other students' work.

Independent Practice Use the On Your Own activity (page 25) as homework or review. Encourage students to use what they have learned in the lesson to complete the assignment. Explain that they can choose an invention from the Idea Box or think of their own idea.

Writing Lessons to Meet the Common Core: Grade 4 © 2013 by Linda Ward Beech, Scholastic Teaching Resources

Name _____ Date _____

A Great Invention

Write about the invention you think is great: the safety pin or the paper clip.

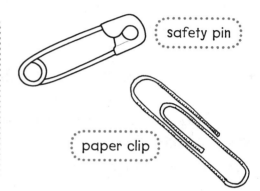

safety pin

paper clip

- Introduce the topic with your audience in mind. Remember to focus on your writing purpose.
- State your opinion and give reasons to support it.
- Organize your reasons and use linking words to connect ideas.
- Write a concluding sentence.
- Write your paragraph on another sheet of paper.

Topic _____

Audience _____

Opinion _____

_____

Supporting Reasons _____

_____

_____

_____

Organizing Information

   Group 1 _____

   _____

   _____

   Group 2 _____

   _____

   _____

Possible Linking Words _____

Concluding Sentence _____

Name _____ Date _____

On Your Own

Choose an invention from the Idea Box or think of one of your own. Complete this page. Then, write a paragraph on another sheet of paper to persuade your classmates that this is a great invention.

Idea Box

○ Scissors   ○ Eraser   ○ Doorknob   ○ My Idea:
_____
_____

Topic _____

Audience _____

Opinion _____

_____

Supporting Reasons _____

_____

_____

_____

Organizing Information

Group 1 _____

_____

_____

Group 2 _____

_____

_____

Possible Linking Words _____

Concluding Sentence _____

_____

Writing Lessons to Meet the Common Core: Grade 4 © 2013 by Linda Ward Beech, Scholastic Teaching Resources

Informative Writing
Hall of Fame

Objectives & Common Core Connections

* Introduce the topic.
* Focus on the purpose of informative writing.
* Conduct research.
* Summarize or paraphrase information in notes.

Introduction Provide each student with a copy of the writing frame (page 27). Read the title and first line. Tell students that they will develop facts for a paragraph about the National Baseball Hall of Fame. Point out that the purpose of informative writing is to inform readers. Explain that it is usually necessary to do research for this kind of writing. Have some relevant books ready.

Model You might say: *The topic is the National Baseball Hall of Fame.* Point out that although page 27 gives some information about this topic, writers can't simply copy it. Stress that when students do research, they must take notes and paraphrase the information by putting it in their own words. Suggest that they look for key words such as *baseball*, *plaques*, and *exhibits* before taking notes. For example:

* baseball—National Hall of Fame in Cooperstown
* plaques—honor 300 people
* exhibits—books, photos, documents, uniforms, equipment

Coach students in developing sentences from their notes. For example:

* The National Baseball Hall of Fame is in Cooperstown, New York.
* A gallery of bronze plaques there honors almost 300 outstanding people in baseball.
* Other displays show baseball-related books, photos, uniforms, and equipment.

Direct students to use the research materials you have assembled to find examples of a player or a manager elected to the Baseball Hall of Fame. Have them record notes. For example:

* Roberto Alomar—second base, elected 2011
* Whitey Herzog—manager, St. Louis Cardinals, elected 2010

Guided Practice Have students complete the writing frame. Encourage them to use their own wording and sentence structure.

Review Invite volunteers to read their notes, sentences, and research to the class. Have listeners use items 1–4 on the assessment checklist (page 63) to evaluate the effectiveness of other students' work.

Independent Practice Use the On Your Own activity (page 28) as homework or review. Encourage students to use what they have learned in the lesson to complete the assignment. Explain that they can choose a hall of fame from the Idea Box or think of one of their own. Have appropriate reference materials and a computer with Internet access available for student research.

Writing Lessons to Meet the Common Core: Grade 4 © 2013 by Linda Ward Beech, Scholastic Teaching Resources

Name _____ Date _____

Hall of Fame

What do you know about the National Baseball Hall of Fame?

- Name the topic.
- Focus on your writing purpose.
- Look for key words.
- Take notes in your own words.
- Write practice sentences from your notes.
- Do your own research to find a player or a manager in the Baseball Hall of Fame. Take notes and write some more practice sentences.

Topic _____

Writing Purpose _____

Sample Text:

The National Baseball Hall of Fame in Cooperstown, New York, has a gallery of bronze plaques to recognize about 300 exceptional figures in baseball. Also exhibited there are books, photos, documents, uniforms, and many examples of baseball equipment.

Key Words _____

_____

Practice Notes _____

_____

_____

Practice Sentences _____

_____

_____

_____

Research and Notes _____

_____

_____

Practice Sentences _____

_____

_____

Writing Lessons to Meet the Common Core: Grade 4 © 2013 by Linda Ward Beech, Scholastic Teaching Resources

Name _____ Date _____

On Your Own

Choose a hall of fame from the Idea Box or think of another one. Complete this page.

Idea Box

○ Basketball Hall of Fame   ○ My Idea: _____

○ Hockey Hall of Fame   _____

○ Football Hall of Fame   _____

Topic _____

Writing Purpose _____

Key Words _____

Research and Notes _____

_____

_____

_____

_____

_____

_____

_____

_____

Practice Sentences _____

_____

_____

_____

_____

Informative Writing
Symbol Story

Introduction Provide each student with a copy of the writing frame (page 30). Have students read the title and first line and study the illustrations. Tell them that they will write an informative paragraph about the bald eagle as a U.S. symbol. Point out that the purpose of this kind of writing is to provide information. Remind students that it is usually necessary to do research for informative writing. Have some relevant books ready.

Model Suggest a sentence to introduce the topic. For example:

* The bald eagle is a symbol of the United States.

Explain that the next step is to develop information using researched facts about the topic. For example:

* on U.S. passports
* represents freedom
* great strength
* on Great Seal

Guide students in grouping these facts and then developing them into sentences. Point out that the first two sentences below are about why the bald eagle was chosen as a symbol, while the third and fourth sentences are about how the eagle is used as a symbol.

* The eagle was chosen for its great strength.
* The soaring eagle also represents freedom.

* The bald eagle appears on the great Seal of the United States.
* You can find the eagle on the cover of a U.S. passport, too.

Guided Practice Have students complete the writing frame. Encourage them to use their own wording and sentence structure.

Review Invite volunteers to read their finished paragraphs to the class. Have listeners use items 1, 2, 4, 5, and 12 on the assessment checklist (page 63) to evaluate the effectiveness of other students' work.

Independent Practice Use the On Your Own activity (page 31) as homework or review. Encourage students to use what they have learned in the lesson to complete the assignment. Explain that they can choose a U.S. symbol from the Idea Box or think of one of their own. Have available appropriate reference materials and a computer with Internet access for student research.

Name _____ Date _____

Symbol Story

What bird is a U.S. symbol?

Great Seal of the U.S.

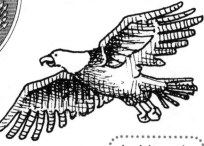

bald eagle

- Introduce the topic.
- Focus on your writing purpose.
- Research, develop, and organize facts.
- Write your paragraph on another sheet of paper.

Topic _____

_____

Writing Purpose _____

_____

Facts _____

_____

_____

_____

_____

_____

Organizing Information

Group 1 _____

_____

_____

Group 2 _____

_____

Writing Lessons to Meet the Common Core: Grade 4 © 2013 by Linda Ward Beech, Scholastic Teaching Resources

Name _____ Date _____

On Your Own

Choose a U.S. symbol from the Idea Box or think of another one. Complete this page. Then, write an informative paragraph on another sheet of paper about the symbol.

Idea Box

○ Flag   ○ Liberty Bell   ○ Statue of Liberty   ○ My Idea:

_____

_____

_____

Topic _____

_____

Writing Purpose _____

_____

Facts _____

_____

_____

_____

_____

Organizing Information

Group 1 _____

_____

_____

Group 2 _____

_____

_____

Explanatory Writing
Money Bunny

Objectives & Common Core Connections

* Introduce the topic for a selected audience.
* Focus on the purpose of explanatory writing.
* List the materials and steps.
* Organize the steps in a logical order.
* Write an explanatory paragraph.
* Include an illustration.

Introduction Provide each student with a copy of the writing frame (page 33). Have students read the title and first line and study the illustrations. Tell them that they will write a paragraph explaining to a younger class how to draw a rabbit. Discuss the purpose of explanatory writing—to inform the reader by telling what, why, or how.

Model Help students begin their explanation by writing an introductory sentence. You might first say: *I need to keep my audience—students in second grade—in mind so I will keep my sentences and directions simple.* For example:

* Here is an easy and fun way to draw a rabbit.

Point out that when explaining how to make or do something, the writer needs to list the materials and steps. For example:

* place the coins in a vertical line with the smallest on top
* get pencil, paper, nickel, dime, quarter
* add ears, face, paws
* trace around the coins

Continue modeling: *I need to organize the steps in a logical way so that readers can follow them.* For example:

* Collect a pencil, paper, nickel, dime, and quarter.
* Line up the coins. Put the dime on top, the nickel in the middle, and the quarter on the bottom.
* Carefully trace around the coins.
* Add ears and a face to the top circle.
* Add two paws to each of the other circles.

Tell students that it is helpful to include illustrations with certain explanations. Discuss how the illustrations on page 33 help a reader know what to do.

Guided Practice Have students complete the writing frame. Encourage them to use their own wording and sentence structure and to draw their own illustrations.

Review Invite volunteers to read their finished paragraphs to the class. Have listeners use items 1, 2, 5, 7–9, and 12 on the assessment checklist (page 63) to evaluate the effectiveness of other students' work.

Independent Practice Use the On Your Own activity (page 34) as homework or review. Encourage students to use what they learned in the lesson to complete the assignment. Tell students they can choose an animal to draw from the Idea Box or think of their own idea. Provide paper so students can draw an illustration to go with their paragraphs.

Writing Lessons to Meet the Common Core: Grade 4 © 2013 by Linda Ward Beech, Scholastic Teaching Resources

Name _____ Date _____

Money Bunny

How can you draw a rabbit?

- Introduce the topic with your audience in mind.
- Focus on your writing purpose.
- List the materials and steps.
- Organize the steps in a logical order.
- Write a paragraph on another sheet of paper to explain how to draw a rabbit.
- Add an illustration to help your readers.

Topic _____

Audience _____

Writing Purpose _____

Materials _____   Steps _____

_____   _____

_____   _____

_____   _____

_____   _____

Steps in Order _____

_____

_____

_____

_____

_____

_____

Name _____ Date _____

On Your Own

Choose an animal to draw from the Idea Box or think of another animal. Complete this page. Then, write a paragraph on another sheet of paper explaining to second graders how to draw the animal. Include an illustration.

Idea Box

○ Dog   ○ Bear   ○ Bird

○ My Idea: _____

Topic _____

Audience _____

Writing Purpose _____

Materials _____   Steps _____

_____   _____

_____   _____

_____   _____

_____   _____

Steps in Order _____

_____

_____

_____

_____

_____

_____

Writing Lessons to Meet the Common Core: Grade 4 © 2013 by Linda Ward Beech, Scholastic Teaching Resources

Explanatory Writing
How to Eat Pizza

Objectives & Common Core Connections

* Introduce the topic for a selected audience.
* Focus on the purpose of explanatory writing.
* List the steps.
* Organize the steps in a logical order.
* Use linking words to connect ideas.
* Write an explanatory paragraph.

Introduction Provide each student with a copy of the writing frame (page 36). Have students read the title and first line and study the illustrations. Tell them that they will write a paragraph explaining to classmates how to eat a slice of pizza.

Model Help students begin their explanation by writing an introductory sentence that would be appropriate for fourth graders. For example:

* It takes skill to eat pizza.

Point out that when explaining how to make or do something, the writer needs to list the steps. For example:

* fold it lengthwise
* put pointed end in mouth
* quickly slurp up filling that oozes out
* wait for it to cool
* take bite

You might say: *I need to organize the steps in a logical way so that readers can follow them.* Coach students in developing complete sentences. Model how some ideas can be connected with linking words, such as *and, also,* or *another*. For example:

* Wait for the pizza to cool.
* Then, fold a slice lengthwise.
* Put the pointed end in your mouth <u>and</u> take a bite.
* Quickly slurp up any topping that oozes out.

Guided Practice Have students complete the writing frame. Encourage them to use their own ideas about eating pizza, as well as their own wording and sentence structure.

Review Invite volunteers to read their finished paragraphs to the class. Have listeners use items 1, 2, 5–7, 9, and 12 on the assessment checklist (page 63) to evaluate the effectiveness of other students' work.

Independent Practice Use the On Your Own activity (page 37) as homework or review. Encourage students to use what they learned in the lesson to complete the assignment. Tell them they can choose a food from the Idea Box or use their own idea.

Writing Lessons to Meet the Common Core: Grade 4 © 2013 by Linda Ward Beech, Scholastic Teaching Resources

Name _____ Date _____

How to Eat Pizza

How do you eat a slice of pizza?

- Introduce the topic with your audience in mind.
- Focus on your writing purpose.
- List the steps.
- Organize the steps in a logical order.
- Use linking words to connect ideas.
- Write a paragraph on another sheet of paper to explain how to eat pizza.

Topic _____

Audience _____

Writing Purpose _____

Steps _____

_____

_____

_____

_____

Steps in Order _____

_____

_____

_____

_____

_____

_____

Possible Linking Words _____

Writing Lessons to Meet the Common Core: Grade 4 © 2013 by Linda Ward Beech, Scholastic Teaching Resources

On Your Own

Choose a food from the Idea Box or think of one of your own. Complete this page. Then, write a paragraph on another sheet of paper to explain how to eat the food.

Idea Box

○ Corn on the Cob   ○ Spaghetti   ○ Ice Pop   ○ My Idea:

_____

_____

_____

Topic _____

Audience _____

Writing Purpose _____

Steps _____

_____

_____

_____

_____

Steps in Order _____

_____

_____

_____

_____

_____

_____

Possible Linking Words _____

Informative Writing
Houses and Homes

Objectives & Common Core Connections

* Introduce the topic for a selected audience.
* Focus on the purpose of informative writing.
* Develop the topic with researched facts and details.
* Use domain-specific words and precise language.
* Use linking words to connect ideas.
* Organize the information to make the topic clear.
* Write an informative paragraph.

Introduction Provide each student with a copy of the writing frame (page 39). Have students read the title and study the illustration. Tell them that they will write a paragraph explaining what a teepee is for an elementary school social studies book. Explain that often it is necessary to do research for informative writing. Have some relevant books ready.

Model Help students begin their explanation by writing an introductory sentence. For example:

* A teepee is a form of shelter used by some Native American groups.

Ask students to think of or find other facts and details that tell what a teepee is. For example:

* easy to assemble
* outside made from buffalo hide
* frame made from poles
* good in high winds
* can be moved to new location

Point out that because you are writing for a social studies book, you are using words such as *shelter* and *location* that are specific to social studies. You are also using precise terms such as *buffalo hide*.

Encourage students to use what they know about organizing information. For instance, two of the details tell what a teepee is made from, while the others explain why a teepee is practical. Coach students in developing complete sentences to use in the paragraph. Model how some ideas can be connected with linking words. For example:

* The outside of a teepee is made from a buffalo hide.
* The hide covers a frame made of long thin poles.
* A teepee is easy to assemble, <u>and</u> it can be moved from one location to another.
* A teepee has a cone shape that helps it stand up well in high winds.

Guided Practice Have students complete the writing frame. Encourage them to use their own wording and sentence structure, and to include other details that they know or have researched about teepees.

Review Call on volunteers to read their finished paragraphs to the class. Have listeners use items 1, 2, 4–6, 9, 10, and 12 on the assessment checklist (page 63) to evaluate the effectiveness of other students' work.

Independent Practice Use the On Your Own activity (page 40) as homework or review. Encourage students to use what they learned in the lesson to complete the assignment. Tell them they can choose a home from the Idea Box or use their own idea. Remind them that they will need to do some research to find facts and details. Have appropriate reference materials and a computer with Internet access available for student research.

Writing Lessons to Meet the Common Core: Grade 4 © 2013 by Linda Ward Beech, Scholastic Teaching Resources

Name _____ Date _____

Houses and Homes

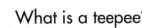

What is a teepee?

- Introduce the topic with your audience in mind.
- Focus on your writing purpose.
- Research and list facts and details about the topic.
- Use social studies words and precise language.
- Use linking words to connect ideas.
- Organize the information to make the topic clear.
- Write your paragraph on another sheet of paper.

Topic _____

Audience _____

Facts and Details _____

_____

_____

_____

_____

_____

Social Studies/Precise Words _____

Possible Linking Words _____

Organizing Information

Group 1 _____

_____

_____

Group 2 _____

_____

Name _____ Date _____

On Your Own

Choose one kind of home from the Idea Box or think of another kind. Complete this page. Then, write a paragraph on another sheet of paper to explain what the home is like.

Idea Box

○ Castle   ○ Houseboat   ○ Igloo   ○ My Idea:
_____
_____

Topic _____

Audience _____

Facts and Details _____

_____

_____

_____

_____

_____

Social Studies/Precise Words _____

Possible Linking Words _____

Organizing Information

Group 1 _____

_____

_____

Group 2 _____

_____

_____

Writing Lessons to Meet the Common Core: Grade 4 © 2013 by Linda Ward Beech, Scholastic Teaching Resources

Informative Writing
Rivers

Objectives & Common Core Connections

* Introduce the topic for a selected audience.
* Focus on the purpose of informative writing.
* Develop the topic with researched facts and details.
* Organize the information to make the topic clear.
* Use linking words to connect ideas.
* Write a concluding sentence.
* Write an informative paragraph.

Introduction Provide each student with a copy of the writing frame (page 42). Have students read the title and first line. Tell them that they will write an informative paragraph about rivers for an elementary grade social studies book. Explain that often it is necessary to do research for informative writing. Have some relevant books ready.

Model Help students begin their text by introducing the topic. For example:

* Rivers are moving bodies of water that flow downhill.

Have students use the reference materials to find other facts and details about rivers. For example:

* water from rainfall, springs, melting snows
* used for transport
* flows through a channel
* provide water for drinking, irrigation
* harness power for electricity

Encourage students to use what they know about organizing information. Point out that some of the information tells what a river is and does

while other facts tell how people use rivers. Coach students in developing complete sentences to use in a paragraph. Model how some ideas can be connected with linking words, such as *also* or *and*. For example:

* River water comes from rainfall, springs, and melting snow and ice.
* A river flows through a channel or path in the land.
* People use rivers for transportation, and they harness the water power to make electricity.
* Rivers also provide water for drinking and irrigation.

Explain that an informative paragraph often has a concluding sentence. For example:

* Rivers are important geographical features.

Guided Practice Have students complete the writing frame. Encourage students to use other facts they have researched about rivers. Provide additional paper for students' paragraphs.

Review Invite volunteers to read their finished paragraphs to the class. Have listeners use items 1, 2, 4–6, 9, 11, and 12 on the assessment checklist (page 63) to evaluate the effectiveness of other students' work.

Independent Practice Use the On Your Own activity (page 43) as homework or review. Encourage students to use what they learned in the lesson to complete the assignment. Tell them that they can choose a geographical feature from the Idea Box or use their own idea. Have appropriate reference materials and a computer with Internet access available for student research.

Name _____ Date _____

Rivers 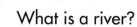 What is a river?

- Introduce the topic with your audience in mind.
- Focus on your writing purpose.
- Research and list facts and details about the topic.
- Use linking words to connect ideas.
- Organize the information to make the topic clear.
- Write a concluding sentence.
- Write your paragraph on another sheet of paper.

Topic _____

Audience _____

Facts and Details _____

_____

_____

_____

Possible Linking Words _____

_____

Organizing Information

   Group 1 _____

_____

_____

   Group 2 _____

_____

_____

Concluding Sentence _____

_____

Name _____ Date _____

On Your Own

Choose a geographical feature from the Idea Box or think of another one. Complete this page. Then, write a paragraph on another sheet of paper telling about the feature.

Idea Box

○ Mountain   ○ Waterfall   ○ Lake   ○ My Idea:

_____

_____

_____

Topic _____

Audience _____

Facts and Details _____

_____

_____

_____

Possible Linking Words _____

_____

Organizing Information

   Group 1 _____

   _____

   _____

   Group 2 _____

   _____

   _____

Concluding Sentence _____

_____

Narrative Writing
A Super Sign

Objectives & Common Core Connections

* Focus on the purpose of narrative writing.
* Establish a situation.
* Establish characters.
* Write a good opening sentence.

Introduction Provide each student with a copy of the writing frame (page 45). Have students read the title and first line. Also discuss the illustration. Ask students what story they think it suggests. Explain to students that they will develop ideas for a narrative based on the picture. Remind them that a narrative is a story or account of something and is usually written to entertain the reader.

Model Point out that a story needs a good beginning so readers will want to continue. Provide an opening sentence related to the illustration. For example:

* Pria saw a sign that gave her a wonderful idea.

Mention that you have given the girl in the illustration a name. Coach students in describing what the illustration shows. For example:

* sign gives Pria idea
* Mother is doubtful
* Pria wants to adopt dog

Guide students in developing the characters and situation. For example:

* Pria really wants a dog. She thinks it would be easy to care for. She wants to go to the dog pound right away and adopt a pet.
* Pria's mom doesn't think Pria knows how much work a dog can be. She's not sure that Pria will always take care of a dog.

Guided Practice Have students complete the writing frame. Encourage them to use their own ideas about the situation and characters. Guide students in developing the situation further by asking: *Do you think Pria's mother will allow Pria to get a dog? Will Pria be a good dog owner? What problems might there be?* Suggest that students develop a narrative about the characters and situation on another sheet of paper. Some students may wish to illustrate their narrative.

Review Invite volunteers to share their finished pages with the class. Have listeners use items 1–4 on the assessment checklist (page 64) to evaluate the effectiveness of other students' work.

Independent Practice Use the On Your Own activity (page 46) as homework or review. Tell students to use what they learned in the lesson to complete the assignment. Explain that they can choose a topic from the Idea Box or use one of their own. Encourage students to include at least two characters and provide a description and background information for each. Provide paper so that students can illustrate their story ideas and characters.

Writing Lessons to Meet the Common Core: Grade 4 © 2013 by Linda Ward Beech, Scholastic Teaching Resources

Name _____ Date _____

A Super Sign

Use the picture to tell a story.

- Focus on your writing purpose.
- Tell what is happening.
- Describe the characters.
- Write a good opening sentence.

Writing Purpose _____

_____

What Is Happening _____

_____

_____

_____

_____

Character 1 _____

_____

_____

Character 2 _____

_____

_____

Opening Sentence _____

_____

_____

Name _____ Date _____

On Your Own

Choose a story topic from the Idea Box or think of one of your own. Complete this page. Draw a picture to go with your story ideas on another sheet of paper.

Idea Box

○ Better Breakfast Month   ○ My Idea: _____

○ National Sports Month   _____

○ National Humor Month   _____

Writing Purpose _____

_____

What Is Happening _____

_____

_____

_____

_____

Character 1 _____

_____

_____

Character 2 _____

_____

_____

Opening Sentence _____

_____

_____

Narrative Writing
Whale Ride

Objectives & Common Core Connections

* Focus on the purpose of narrative writing.
* Establish a situation and a character.
* Write a good opening sentence.
* Address the audience appropriately.
* Organize the events in order.
* Write a narrative.

Introduction Provide each student with a copy of the writing frame (page 48). Discuss the title and illustrations. Tell students that they will use the illustrations to develop a narrative for fourth graders. Review that a narrative is a story or account of something and is usually written to entertain the reader.

Model Summarize the situation in the illustrations and discuss the character. You might say: *A boy goes to the beach and falls asleep. He dreams he is riding on a whale. When he wakes up, he sees picture of a whale on his towel.* Model a sentence to begin the narrative. Explain that you want it to appeal to fourth graders. For example:

* Lars was looking forward to an exciting time at the beach.

Mention that you have given the boy in the illustrations a name. Coach students in describing what the pictures show. For example:

* arrives at beach
* dreams he's on whale
* wakes up confused
* sees whale on beach towel

Remind students that a narrative has a beginning, middle, and end. Review the sequence of events in the illustrations. Work with students to develop complete sentences and organize the events.

* Lars unpacked his towel.
* The warm sun made him sleepy.
* He dreamed he was riding on a whale!
* He wasn't riding on a whale, but he was sleeping on one!

Guided Practice Have students complete the writing frame. Encourage them to use their own ideas about the situation and character. Point out that students can include additional characters.

Review Invite volunteers to share their finished pages with the class. Have listeners use items 1–6 and 11 on the assessment checklist (page 64) to evaluate the effectiveness of other students' work.

Independent Practice Use the On Your Own activity (page 49) as homework or review. Tell students to use what they learned in the lesson to complete the assignment. Explain that they can choose a topic from the Idea Box or use one of their own. Provide additional paper and invite students to include at least two illustrations to support their narratives. Also suggest that they include a title.

Whale Ride

Use the pictures to tell a story.

- Focus on your writing purpose and keep your audience in mind.
- Tell what is happening and describe any characters.
- Write a good opening sentence.
- Organize the events in order.
- Write your narrative on another sheet of paper.

Writing Purpose _____

Audience _____

What Is Happening _____

_____

_____

_____

Character(s) _____

_____

Opening Sentence _____

_____

Order of Events _____

_____

_____

_____

Name _____ Date _____

On Your Own

Choose a story topic from the Idea Box or think of one of your own. Complete this page. Write your narrative on another sheet of paper. You might include two or more illustrations that support your story.

Idea Box

○ A Ride on an Eagle   ○ My Idea: _____

○ A Ride on a Zebra   _____

○ A Ride on a Cheetah   _____

Writing Purpose _____

Audience _____

What Is Happening _____

_____

_____

_____

_____

Character(s) _____

_____

Opening Sentence _____

_____

Order of Events _____

_____

_____

_____

Narrative Writing
Where Is It?

Objectives & Common Core Connections

* Focus on the purpose of narrative writing.
* Establish a situation and characters.
* Write a good opening sentence.
* Address the audience appropriately.
* Organize the events in order.
* Use dialogue.
* Write a narrative.

Introduction Provide each student with a copy of the writing frame (page 51). Discuss the title and illustrations. Tell students that they will use the illustrations to develop a narrative for fourth graders. Review that a narrative is a story or account of something and is usually written to entertain the reader.

Model Summarize the situation in the illustrations and discuss the characters. You might say: *A girl is eating breakfast, and her mother reminds her to take her homework to school. The girl looks everywhere but can't find it. The bus comes, and she leaves. At school, she unpacks her backpack, and there is her homework.* Model a sentence to begin the narrative. Explain that you want it to appeal to fourth graders. For example:

* Su Lin was sometimes disorganized in the morning.

Mention that you have given the girl in the illustrations a name. Coach students in describing what the pictures show. For example:

* girl eating breakfast
* looks everywhere

* gets on bus
* unpacks backpack and finds homework

Draw attention to the speech balloons and point out that a writer uses dialogue to show how a character feels or responds to an event. For example:

* "Don't forget your homework, Su Lin."
* "It was right here. What happened to it?"

Review the sequence of events in the illustrations. Work with students to develop complete sentences about the events. For example:

* The bus came, and Su Lin got on without finding her homework.
* At school she emptied her backpack, and there it was.
* "My homework was here all along. Phew!"

Guided Practice Have students complete the writing frame. Encourage them to use their own dialogue. Be sure to review how to use capitalization and punctuation in dialogue.

Review Invite volunteers to share their finished pages with the class. Have listeners use items 1–7 and 11 on the assessment checklist (page 64) to evaluate the effectiveness of other students' work.

Independent Practice Use the On Your Own activity (page 52) as homework or review. Tell students to use what they learned in the lesson to complete the assignment. Explain that they can choose a topic from the Idea Box or use one of their own. Remind students to include at least two characters to make the use of dialogue realistic. Also suggest that they title their finished narratives.

Where Is It?

Use the pictures to tell a story.

- Focus on your writing purpose.
- Think about your audience.
- Tell what is happening and describe the characters.
- Write a good opening sentence.
- Organize the events in order.
- Use dialogue to make the story clear.
- Write your narrative on another sheet of paper.

Writing Purpose/Audience _____

What Is Happening _____

_____

_____

Character 1 _____ Character 2 _____

Opening Sentence _____

_____

Order of Events _____

_____

_____

_____

Dialogue _____

_____

_____

_____

Name _____ Date _____

On Your Own

Choose a story topic from the Idea Box or think of one of your own. Complete this page. Then, write your narrative on another sheet of paper.

Idea Box

○ The Lost Baseball Glove   ○ My Idea: _____

○ The Lost Library Book   _____

○ The Lost Violin Bow   _____

Writing Purpose/Audience _____

What Is Happening _____

_____

_____

Character 1 _____

Character 2 _____

Opening Sentence _____

_____

Order of Events _____

_____

_____

_____

Dialogue _____

_____

_____

_____

Writing Lessons to Meet the Common Core: Grade 4 © 2013 by Linda Ward Beech, Scholastic Teaching Resources

Narrative Writing
Full Moon

Objectives & Common Core Connections

* Focus on the purpose of narrative writing for a selected audience.
* Establish a situation and characters.
* Write a good opening sentence.
* Organize the events in order.
* Use sensory words.
* Write a narrative.

Introduction Provide each student with a copy of the writing frame (page 54). Discuss the title, first line, and illustrations. Tell students that they will use the illustrations to develop a narrative for a magazine audience. Review that a narrative is a story or account of something and is usually written to entertain the reader.

Model Summarize the situation in the illustrations and discuss what the characters are doing. You might say: *A man and his son are driving at night. They stop by the road to gaze at a full moon. Maybe they can hear an owl hooting as they gaze at the sky.* Model a sentence to begin the narrative. For example:

* There was a full moon when Eli and his dad drove home from the movies.

Mention that you have given the boy in the illustrations a name. Coach students in describing what the pictures show. For example:

* stop car and get out
* owl nearby
* moon lights up landscape
* mystery of night

Explain that you want to use sensory words that capture the scene and show how the characters feel. For example:

* owl's haunting call
* pale glow
* painted the landscape
* stood silently

Work with students to develop complete sentences and organize the events. For example:

* Dad stopped the car, and they got out to look.
* The moon's light painted the landscape in a pale glow.
* Nearby they heard the haunting call of an owl.
* Dad and Eli stood silently taking in the mystery of the night.

Guided Practice Have students complete the writing frame. Encourage them to use their own sensory words.

Review Invite volunteers to share their finished pages with the class. Have listeners use items 1–6, 8, and 11 on the assessment checklist (page 64) to evaluate the effectiveness of other students' work.

Independent Practice Use the On Your Own activity (page 55) as homework or review. Encourage students to use what they learned in the lesson to complete the assignment. Explain that they can choose a topic from the Idea Box or use one of their own. Also suggest that students title their finished narratives.

Full Moon

What's it like when the moon is full?

- Focus on your writing purpose.
- Think about your audience.
- Tell what is happening and describe the characters.
- Write a good opening sentence.
- Organize the events in order.
- Use sensory words.
- Write your narrative on another sheet of paper.

Writing Purpose _____

Audience _____

What Is Happening _____

_____

_____

_____

Character 1 _____ Character 2 _____

Opening Sentence _____

_____

Order of Events _____

_____

_____

_____

Sensory Words _____

_____

Name _____ Date _____

On Your Own

Choose a story topic from the Idea Box or think of one of your own. Complete this page. Then, write your narrative on another sheet of paper.

Idea Box

○ A Sunrise

○ Top of a Mountain

○ Before a Storm

○ My Idea: _____

_____

_____

Writing Purpose _____

Audience _____

What Is Happening _____

_____

_____

_____

Character 1 _____

Character 2 _____

Opening Sentence _____

_____

Order of Events _____

_____

_____

_____

Sensory Words _____

_____

_____

Narrative Writing
Mrs. Bean's Shoes

Objectives & Common Core Connections

* Establish characters and a situation.
* Write a good opening sentence.
* Organize the events in order.
* Use transitional words.
* Use dialogue.
* Write a narrative.

Introduction Provide each student with a copy of the writing frame (page 57). Discuss the title, first line, and illustrations. Tell students that they will use the illustrations to develop a narrative. Remind them that a narrative can be about a real or, as in this lesson, an imagined event.

Model Summarize the situation in the illustrations and point out that the characters are shoes. You might say: *A pair of shoes goes for a walk and has some problems. They decide it's better to walk with someone in them.* Model a sentence to begin a narrative. For example:

* Mrs. Bean's shoes decided to go for a walk without her.

Coach students in describing what the illustrations suggest. For example:

* don't stay together so one shoe gets lost
* boy steps on one shoe
* dog tries to grab shoe
* go home

Work with students to develop complete sentences and organize the events. Point out that a writer often uses transitional words, such as *first, next, then,* and *after,* to manage the pacing of events. For example:

* A boy stepped on Right Shoe because he didn't see it.
* Then, Left Shoe got lost because the shoes didn't stay together.
* Next, a dog tried to run away with Right Shoe.
* After that, the shoes decided to go home.

Remind students that they can use dialogue to show what their characters are thinking. For example:

* "It's no good walking without Mrs. Bean," said Left Shoe.

Guided Practice Have students complete the writing frame. Encourage them to use their own transitional words and dialogue.

Review Invite volunteers to share their finished narratives with the class. Have listeners use items 2–4, 6, 7, 9, and 11 on the assessment checklist (page 64) to evaluate the effectiveness of other students' work.

Independent Practice Use the On Your Own activity (page 58) as homework or review. Encourage students to use what they learned in the lesson to complete the assignment. Tell them that they can choose a topic from the Idea Box or one of their own. Provide additional paper and invite students to illustrate their narratives. Also suggest that they include a title.

Writing Lessons to Meet the Common Core: Grade 4 © 2013 by Linda Ward Beech, Scholastic Teaching Resources

Name _____ Date _____

Mrs. Bean's Shoes

⭐ What happens when shoes
go walking by themselves?

- Tell what is happening and describe the characters.
- Write a good opening sentence.
- Organize the events in order.
- Use transitional words.
- Use dialogue to make the story clear.
- Write your narrative on another sheet of paper.

What Is Happening _____

_____

_____

Character 1 _____

Character 2 _____

Opening Sentence _____

_____

Order of Events _____

_____

_____

_____

_____

Transitional Words _____

Dialogue _____

_____

Name _____ Date _____

On Your Own

Choose a story topic from the Idea Box or think of one of your own. Complete the page. Then, write your narrative on another sheet of paper.

Idea Box

○ Skis Without Skier   ○ My Idea: _____

○ Flippers Without Diver   _____

○ Skates Without Skater   _____

What Is Happening _____

_____

_____

Character 1 _____

Character 2 _____

Opening Sentence _____

_____

Order of Events _____

_____

_____

_____

Transitional Words _____

Dialogue _____

_____

_____

Narrative Writing
Cat Nap

Objectives & Common Core Connections

* Establish characters and a situation.
* Write a good opening sentence.
* Organize the events and use transitional words.
* Use dialogue.
* Write a concluding sentence.
* Write a narrative.

Introduction Provide each student with a copy of the writing frame (page 60). Discuss the title, first line, and illustrations. Tell students that they will use the illustrations to develop a narrative. Remind them that a narrative can be about a real or an imagined event.

Model Summarize the situation in the illustrations. You might say: *A girl makes her bed and then goes to school. Her cat gets in bed and plays. Later, the girl and her mother find the messy bed. Cat feels guilty and goes to hide.* Model a sentence to begin a narrative. For example:

* Eva promised to make her bed every day if her parents would let her have a cat.

Point out that you have given the girl in the illustrations a name. Coach students in interpreting what the pictures show. For example:

* Eva makes bed and leaves
* her cat plays in bed
* see messy bed
* guilty cat

Work with students to develop complete sentences and organize the events. Invite them

to give the cat a name. Remind them that they can use dialogue to show what the characters are thinking and transitional words to pace events. For example:

* One day, Eva made her bed as usual and <u>then</u> left for school.
* Along came Tiger. "That's a good place to play."
* When Eva came home, her mother pointed to her bed and said, "Eva, you made a promise."
* Very quietly, Tiger slipped away.

Point out that a good narrative usually has an ending or conclusion. For example:

* "I guess I should learn how to make a bed," thought Tiger.

Guided Practice Have students complete the writing frame. Encourage them to use their own dialogue and concluding sentence.

Review Invite volunteers to share their finished narratives with the class. Have listeners use items 2–4, 6, 7, and 9–11 on the assessment checklist (page 64) to evaluate the effectiveness of other students' work.

Independent Practice Use the On Your Own activity (page 61) as homework or review. Encourage students to use what they learned in the lesson to complete the assignment. Tell them that they can choose a topic from the Idea Box or one of their own. Remind students that they should include three characters in their narratives. Also suggest that they include a title.

Name _____ Date _____

Cat Nap 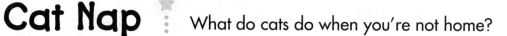 What do cats do when you're not home?

- Tell what is happening and describe the three characters.
- Write a good opening sentence.
- Organize the events in order.
- Use transitional words.
- Use dialogue to make the story clear.
- Write a concluding sentence.
- Write your narrative on another sheet of paper.

What Is Happening _____

_____

_____

Character 1   Character 2   Character 3

_____   _____   _____

Opening Sentence _____

_____

Order of Events _____

_____

_____

_____

Transitional Words _____

Dialogue _____

_____

Concluding Sentence _____

_____

Name _____   Date _____

On Your Own

Choose a story topic about a misbehaving pet from the Idea Box or think of one of your own. Complete this page. Then, write your narrative on another sheet of paper.

Idea Box

○ Pesky Parrot   ○ My Idea: _____

○ Runaway Rabbit   _____

○ Messy Mouse   _____

What Is Happening _____

_____

_____

Character 1   Character 2   Character 3

_____   _____   _____

Opening Sentence _____

_____

Order of Events _____

_____

_____

_____

Transitional Words _____

Dialogue _____

_____

Concluding Sentence _____

_____

Name _____ Date _____

Student Assessment Checklist
Opinion Writing

1. Introduced the topic. .... ☐

2. Focused on the writing purpose. .... ☐

3. Stated an opinion. .... ☐

4. Developed and presented reasons, facts, and/or details
to support an opinion. .... ☐

5. Organized the reasons, facts, and/or details
in a logical order. .... ☐

6. Connected the reasons and opinion with linking words. .... ☐

7. Addressed the audience appropriately. .... ☐

8. Provided a concluding sentence. .... ☐

9. Wrote a paragraph that offers an opinion. .... ☐

More Things to Check

- Capitalized proper nouns. ☐
- Capitalized the first word of sentences. ☐
- Used correct punctuation. ☐
- Spelled words correctly. ☐
- Followed correct paragraph form. ☐

Name _____ Date _____

Student Assessment Checklist
Informative/Explanatory Writing

1. Introduced the topic. .... ☐

2. Focused on the writing purpose. .... ☐

3. Summarized or paraphrased information in notes. .... ☐

4. Developed topic using researched facts, examples, and/or details. .... ☐

5. Organized the information to help the reader. .... ☐

6. Used linking words to connect ideas. .... ☐

7. Listed materials and steps. .... ☐

8. Included an illustration to aid comprehension. .... ☐

9. Addressed the audience appropriately. .... ☐

10. Used subject-specific words and precise language. .... ☐

11. Provided a concluding sentence. .... ☐

12. Wrote an informative/explanatory paragraph. .... ☐

More Things to Check

- Capitalized proper nouns. ☐
- Capitalized the first word of sentences. ☐
- Used correct punctuation. ☐
- Spelled words correctly. ☐
- Followed correct paragraph form. ☐

Writing Lessons to Meet the Common Core: Grade 4 © 2013 by Linda Ward Beech, Scholastic Teaching Resources

Name _____   Date _____

Student Assessment Checklist
Narrative Writing

1. Focused on the writing purpose. .... ☐

2. Established the situation. .... ☐

3. Established real or imagined characters. .... ☐

4. Developed a good opening sentence. .... ☐

5. Addressed the audience appropriately. .... ☐

6. Organized the events in sequence. .... ☐

7. Included dialogue. .... ☐

8. Used sensory words. .... ☐

9. Used transitional words. .... ☐

10. Provided a conclusion. .... ☐

11. Wrote a narrative. .... ☐

More Things to Check

- Capitalized proper nouns. ☐

- Capitalized the first word of sentences. ☐

- Used correct punctuation. ☐

- Spelled words correctly. ☐

- Followed correct paragraph form. ☐

Writing Lessons to Meet the Common Core: Grade 4 © 2013 by Linda Ward Beech, Scholastic Teaching Resources